Pieces of Me

A collection of poems and short stories

JORDAN FREELS

TYMM PUBLISHING LLC
COLUMBIA, SC

Pieces of Me: A collection of poems and short stories
Copyright © 2018 Jordan Freels

ALL RIGHTS RESERVED.

No part of this book may be reproduced or transmitted in any form or by any means, electronic or mechanical, including photocopying, recording, or by any information storage or retrieval system, without permission in writing from the Publisher.

Paperback ISBN: 978-0-692-08659-9

Publishing Assistance: Tymm Publishing LLC
Cover Artwork: Karae Coursey
Copy Editing: Barbara Joe, Amani Publishing, LLC

Pieces of Me

Dedication

Thank you to my family for always loving, believing, supporting, pushing, and encouraging me. I hope I've made all of you proud. To my forever angels: Uncle Michael and Grandma, I love you.

Contents

Introduction 1

Part I.
Old Love

My Perfect Person 5

Sweet Chocolate 9

One Year 11

Beating Hearts 15

Our Dark Love 17

My Darkness 19

Letter 1 21

Letter 2 23

Letter 3 27

Letter 4 29

Letter 5 31

Letter 6 33

Letter 7 35

Letter 8 37

Euphoria 39

Forces 41

My Heart is Still Broken 43

A Healing Heart 45

Empty 49

Part II.
Who am I?

It's All About Me 55

It Makes Me Sick 59

Cold Hearted 63

Color Me 65

Running Thoughts 71

Fatherless Man 73

Living Silently 83

Tired 85

Masterpieces 89

Same Old Same Old 93

Part III.
Love Is

Love Is 97

Simple Chick   99

Secret   103

Life Lessons   107

Stereotypical Love   109

That Special One   113

Being What We Want to Be   117

726   119

Bare Skin   123

Fairy Tale   125

Hopeful   129

Dream Chasing   131

Reflections About My Best Friend   135

A Beautiful Mind   139

I Wish   141

Dear Black Man   143

Before It Even Began   145

One Accord   147

Shattered Sunshine   149

Part IV.
Short Stories

Character 1   155

Character 2   157

Character 3 161

About the Author 165

Introduction

It has been my dream to write this book. I wrote it to inspire and let others know it's okay to not always be happy; there will be moments when things just aren't right. While a good majority of my work is about love, I also touch on feeling neglected and coping with not having a relationship with my biological father; my feelings of heartache, pain, and sadness and what past, current, and future relationships mean to me. Understand there is some strong content with some of these pieces, and they were written in a time of hurt.

Pieces of Me is my life, it's a blueprint of me. It is my outlet for expressing how I feel in the most honest way. I hope my book gives readers the opportunity to learn a little bit about me, and themselves. My desire is that my book gives someone the inspiration to write and express how they feel in a way they never knew they could.

Pieces of Me is validation that I am a skilled writer. It is my first book of many. I hope you enjoy.

PART I
Old Love

My Perfect Person

8/28/09

I never would have thought meeting you would change my life completely.

You're the "perfect" person to me. I put perfect in quotations because there is no real definition. If there were, you'd be it. You have opened up my eyes and taught me so many things. I don't know what I would do without you.

I constantly have you on my mind. I never would have thought you and I would be together, but I'm happy because we're like a puzzle.

We fit "perfectly."

You make me feel so different than I've ever felt. I can see us growing old together and still having the same feelings from many years before.

A, I love you for so many different reasons and telling you every reason why would be the only correct way to express myself to you.

I love you because you accept me for me. I love you because you treat me how I should be treated. I love you because I get butterflies in my stomach whenever we hang out. I love you because you're making something of yourself and you're helping me along the way. I love you because you're not afraid to get emotional in front of me or tell me how much you love me. I love you because you tell me I'm beautiful all the time, and I never get tired of hearing it. I love you because you do things for me others wouldn't. I love you because I feel safe with you, and I know I can turn to you if I ever need anything. I love you because when you stare at me, I get a warm feeling inside. In my heart, I know you love me just as much, and that feeling is absolutely "perfect."

You are

My soulmate.

My everything.

My heart.

PIECES OF ME

You are the "perfect" person for me.

I love you.

Sweet Chocolate

2/16/10

Baby, I'm glad you're my valentine.
You are my sweet chocolate.
You make my heart melt every time you kiss me.
You make me hot when you flirt with me.
You are my sweet chocolate.
You have my heart, and I have yours.
You are my sweet chocolate.
I know you'll soon be my husband.
You are my sweet chocolate.
I love you.
Sweet Chocolate.

One Year

7/29/10

Baby,

I love you.

We've had our ups and downs, but there is so much I am grateful for because of you.

One year of laughs.

One year of cries.

One year of long talks.

Every memory we've shared, I cherish every day because we've been together.

One year of I love you's.

One year of I miss you's.

Jordan Freels

One year of family functions spent together.

Not a day goes by when I don't think about you or how I wish I could see you and spend time with you.

Our year together has made us stronger, and everyone can see it.

A year with you is breathtaking because we've experienced so much together as a couple;

I know we'll experience much more.

One year of silly faces.

One year of memories.

One year of happiness.

I see myself with you forever until the day I die.

The more we talk about our lives together, the faster I want it to be true. So we can live happily with our own family and each other's family as well.

I see us being happier as we grow older from the happiness we give each other now because we will have matured more and have a greater understanding of everything around us.

I wish the best for us and the best for you because when you are not happy, neither am I. When you are upset, I am upset. When you are feeling down and stressed, so am I. But I know the one emotion neither of us can run out of is love.

Baby, I love you. We've had an amazing year, and I know there will be more to follow.

One year of happiness.

One year of love.

Beating Hearts

10/24/10

Words can't describe the feelings I have for you.

You give me chills when you kiss me; when I feel your hands wrap around my body.

I crave your scent and the way you make my body feel.

You tease me, and it drives me insane.

Your demeanor is a turn on; it makes me understand you'll have my back.

You love me unconditionally.

I need to have you as my husband so we can grow, love, learn, and laugh with each other.

The day we die, our spirits will still live on through our children, through our families.

Jordan Freels

Through the beat of each other's hearts because we became one.

I love you.

2:34 a.m.

Our Dark Love

11/3/10

I wonder who we are as a whole.

We struggle, and we fight.

Our love is stronger than the dark hole we've succumbed to.

You captivate me, and I wonder if you feel the same.

We shed more tears than the most treacherous rainstorm; yet we still put the biggest smile on each other's faces.

How is it that we fight to the death, but we can love so deeply the pain is pleasurable?

This dark state we've become used to is not the end for us, and the reason I know is because I believe true love conquers all...

Jordan Freels

The question is, do you?

My Darkness

11/3/10

I feel empty without you by my side.

Lonely. Depressed. Afraid. Dazed.

When will you be by my side again?

You never leave my memory.

I need you so that I can be joyful again.

Happiness. Solitude.

Writing this poem is painful because of all the hurt I feel.

Only you can bring me true happiness.

These words numb my pain, but only you can make me whole again.

Jordan Freels

I know one day we will be together again, and when that day comes, I will no longer feel.

Alone and in the dark.

10:00 p.m.

Letter 1

11/7/10

Dear You:

So, there's this guy; I miss him. I wonder if he misses me and if he's even thought about me since our last encounter. I haven't been able to get him out of my head. Yeah, it's you I'm talking about. You're the only one for me baby. The only one I need.

From,

This girl you want to be your wife.

Letter 2

11/17/10

Dear You:

I'm not even sure why I've decided to write you a letter. I haven't cried in days; and today, I just got really sad thinking about you. I think I'll write you a letter every day to see how it makes me feel. If I'll feel any better because this not talking to you, is difficult. I thought this was a good move. But as I've told you, seeing your BBM (Blackberry Messenger) and Facebook statuses, I can't help but wonder. Do some of my BBM statuses make you wonder if they're about you? But then I feel like why should it matter? I've become paranoid about what you do, and I don't understand why. I guess it is part of the process, but I honestly don't know. I wonder what you're doing and if you've even thought about contacting me. I thought talking to other people would help me; I thought that would be my way of not thinking about you or us. For a while, it worked. But for whatever reason, I just started crying today.

When I say, "talk to other people," I mean my friends. Please, don't get any ideas because I'd never do that, I'd never talk to another male to distract myself out of spite so I won't think about you so much. I'm tired of crying, and I'm tired of feeling how I do. I honestly haven't thought about you so much because I guess I'm in your stage now, not thinking about you because it is too painful. Please don't take offense to anything I say because I'm just expressing myself differently, seeing if this will help me. I love you, and I always will. But just today, I've thought what if things don't work out how we want. All these bad thoughts used to come in my head when we first broke up, and I was so scared something was going to happen to you. It was so hard for me not to call you and make sure you were okay. I wonder if your Blackberry Messenger statuses are sometimes about me or if you're doing it to be spiteful. I don't know anything really. I feel so clouded right now; it's insane. I wonder how you're going to take these letters and what I write because one day, I'd like to show them to you. Sorry, if I repeated myself already. I wonder if things are going to change between us if we get back together.

I know I'll feel awkward around your family all over again. I do know what I plan to do for us to make us better, happier, and stronger.

Tomorrow, I have my creative writing class. I'll be sharing my poem, "Red Zone." Let's hope I don't break down. I can't take that in class. I just lost my train of thought, and I was really on a roll. I hope you're doing okay; it sure seems like it. This letter has helped a little bit. Let's see what tomorrow holds. I wonder if you've thought about dating other people since we're not together anymore. While an older friend, role model, suggested it to me, I told her that's not what we want. I don't want it. I hope you don't, either. But if that's what you decide, just know you'll crush me even more and getting over you will be even harder. I'll be scorned for a while, hypothetically speaking, of course, if we don't get back together because of whatever reason. I got this weird feeling in my brain the other day, and I got scared because I wanted to turn to you, but I couldn't. Let's see what day three has in store for you.

From,

Me.

Letter 3

11/18/10

Dear You:

Today is a better day. Haven't thought about you much. It seems as if things are getting easier for me. Hope all is well for you. Today, I'll be going to the movies with Jasmine. I'm excited because it's just another day I won't think about you. I'm still not sure how to write these letters or what to say, but I think it'll help me. Today's the first Thursday I won't be leaving with you, and it feels weird. I'm ending this letter now, and I might start up later if I can think of something to say. I did not even get a chance to read my poem because my class was cancelled.

From,

Me.

# Letter 4

11/19/10

Dear You:

I hope your day was okay. After speaking to a friend, whom I consider a role model, she got me thinking. I don't know if I want to think like this. She says you might end up dating people first. While I wouldn't want that, I'm not sure where your mind is at. I want to ask you so bad, but I can't because of what I promised myself, and I'm truly scared of what your answer might be. I would hope I know you well enough where I would know you wouldn't, but I'm honestly not sure because my mind is not yours. I enjoyed myself last night with my friends, and I'm enjoying myself today. Haven't thought about you so much, trying not to, but because of what I just told you, I have been. Each day gets easier for me. I am tired of thinking about you it is driving me crazy. I feel like me trying to change for myself is worth it but doing it without you is killing me. As much as I hang with my friends, I feel like it is not worth it. If you were to date another girl, I'd be crushed. I really would become numb to being hurt; I would not allow myself to be with anyone for years because of how hurt I'd be. This, right now, is the hardest letter for me to write. That's all for now.

From,

Me.

Letter 5

11/20/10

Dear You:

Finally, I feel better knowing my paranoia was just me. We talked today about how things are, and we've come to the decision that we don't want to be with each other because right now is not the right time. While I was a bit hurt about how you said it, I am fine. I feel free. I will always love you, and I want to be with you when the time is right. But, right now, it is not working out. So, I won't be talking to you for a while. You don't like talking to me, so you say, and I don't mind it.

It is hard because you are like my best friend, but I think it'll get easier for me. I think dating other people could help us if we choose to later down the road, but I am not ready for that. If you do before me, I think I'll be over you by then. If not, I can't do anything but accept you are happy and that you've moved on and found someone who can treat you better. I can dance, flirt, and do whatever I want now. Not saying I'm just doing it out of spite, but I feel so free. I like this feeling, and while I still do love you, it is best.

From,

Me.

Letter 6

11/21/10

Dear You:

I spoke to you today. Tired of crying over you. I hate it. You asked for the ring back. I wish you hadn't because you gave it to me, but it's what you want. Wish time was on my side because I'm tired of thinking about you. You drink a lot more now; that's funny. Enjoy your life and your new freedom. I'm sick of it. Just everything. Deleting you from my Blackberry Messenger and Facebook was a thought, but whenever I decide to talk to you, you should be there if you're not in the academy by then. If you even want to talk to me, since you said yourself you like not talking to me. Nice. Just sick of it all. It's hard not thinking about you, but I'm going to try my hardest because I can't take it anymore. You're not thinking about me, so why should I waste my energy?

From,

Me.

Letter 7

11/22/10

Dear You:

You were rarely on my mind today. I enjoyed my day. I can finally say I'm over you as far as not thinking about you so much. I have other things on my mind. Glad I have my friends and other things to keep me occupied. That's all I can do. Who knows how far this letter business will go? Even though I think I told you I'd like to write you every day, who knows now. Officially done crying over you. And talking about you isn't so hard. I just get to the gist of the things and keep it moving. I couldn't be happier.

From,

Me.

Letter 8

11/24/10

Dear You:

I missed a day of writing to you, and I was okay with that. Seeing you today was alright. When you kissed me on the cheek, I wasn't expecting that again since the first time you did it was when I returned the sneakers to you. You're only in my head because I saw you, but I am vaguely thinking about you or what you're doing. I feel free. I am not the same as I was a couple of days ago. I'm sure you can tell my attitude has changed by reading these letters. Who knows?

From,

Me.

P.S. I wonder if I miss you. I honestly don't know, and it's probably because I'm trying my hardest not to think about you. I'm sure when the time comes, and we start to talk again, the feelings will come back. I'm not saying that they've gone; but, right now, they're hidden because I'm trying to focus on me. I do not think my feelings for you will ever go away unless things change between us and that I do not want. You already know. I love you.

Euphoria

12/8/10

My euphoria is not your average high.

It is simply words on a page.

A book.

To read other humans' words entrances me because I feel as if I'm a character.

I get lost in the words like little girls get lost in the world of drugs, and sometimes the little girls in the books do.

They're coerced into believing the men taking care of them are going to love and support them like my family does. But although the characters are fictional, the situations they go through are real.

I'm fortunate to be loved and cherished by so many

that only the words succumb me into a state of ecstasy and not actually partake in the drug itself.

My euphoria gets me high ... high ... high ... the more and more I turn the pages, I'm sucked into the characters' stories.

While the characters in these stories are fake, I'm the main character in my world.

Forces

12/8/10

Two forces are surrounding me, and I like this feeling.

I know so much about one but nothing of the other.

His laugh makes me laugh, and his I've never heard.

I know him like the back of my hand. I know I want him to be mine.

His style is a plus, and his is unknown to me.

I wonder if these feelings for you are real, or do I just want to feel how I feel about this mystery guy.

I wish I weren't pulled in either direction because I'm unsure where to go.

I've grown to like you, and my attraction to him has diminished because he is too unknown to me. While this was my immediate attraction to him, I can no longer see him as a possible partner.

We talk constantly, you and I, and because he and I talk so minimally, there is no connection.

The attraction we have for one another overpowers anything he and I could ever have because he is too complex. I feel as though the secrets he has would never allow us to be anything more than friends. But with you, I feel as if there is a greater possibility.

Can there be a medium we can agree to?

I feel as if this medium is not even needed because the force on the left is who's constantly on my mind; while the force on the right is just an afterthought.

My Heart is Still Broken

12/22/10

Your memory is still within me.

To be asked how you are pains me, because I'm still struggling not to think of you.

I feel as if I'm doing good, but the simple mention of your name makes me want to curl into a ball.

Why is this not getting easier like I feel it should?

I'm tired of you being in my thoughts because we aren't one. We've moved on, and while I've been happy, I need to be able to hear your name and not feel so weak. I don't want you to have this hold on me because you're not the significant other I wanted you to be.

I question if I'll have the fairy tale story I want; I want you to be my husband, my all. I struggle to think if you feel the same, and I question if it'll be love everlasting. I fight myself every day because I want to talk to you, but I feel like you'd brush me off. Who knows? This time apart I hope helps because I feel as if you're my soulmate.

I hope we're right because while I'm doing me, I'm still stuck when I wanna be completely free.

I'm still not breathing correctly.

I need you to revive me.

Please.

Signed,

My Heart is Still Broken.

A Healing Heart

12/22/10

These thoughts I have of you being the only person to make me breathe correctly is preposterous.

While not having you as my partner pains me, I should not feel the need to depend on you to bring me life again.

Only I can bring me life, but it's hard to become happy when the person I've known for so long can do that so perfectly.

You.

You are the one. At least that's how I feel, but how you were with me makes me wonder if you'll still be the same.

You weren't necessarily controlling me, but you did have a hold on me, not feeling comfortable with me dancing and feeling as if I always changed my story. Who knows if that'll ever change? If we are meant to be, I hope this time apart would show me that you've grown. While you never had a problem trusting me, it was the other guys you felt insecure about. That needs to stop.

I cannot be with someone who feels like dancing is a problem. If there cannot be a compromise, then I'll have to be set free … again … I'm fine with that feeling. While it'll hurt me because I feel you are the one, I want to live my life and enjoy it. Just like you are, and you did, but I never stopped you from doing things you liked.

I never quite understood how you felt I would change my story. I never wanted to make you angry purposely, but you did not see that the words I would tell you were the truth. I would not twist them to make you think one thing when I was doing another. In my head, it was normal. You say one thing, but you mean another. How could I possibly do such a thing to hurt you? Me? The one person who was always there for you, purposely hurt your feelings, no, not me. I don't have that much brain power to deceive you.

I loved you with all my heart, still do. I find it odd

how we're supposed to be "friends," but we don't talk. Maybe this is part of the process because it was me who said I'd talk to you when I was ready, and you have yet to see how your "friend" is doing.

So, I've decided to stick to my word because you're obviously not putting in the effort. Cool. No one's forcing you. It would be nice to hear from you, but my opinion doesn't matter anymore. The ball is in your court; I'm tired of playing this game alone.

I now realize I no longer need the life you gave me. I need to be happy for me first.

Only me.

Signed,

A *Healing Heart*.

Empty

4/15/12

My emptiness consumes me, and sometimes it consumes me to where I must shed tears.

Why?

I am beautiful. I am intelligent.

So why should I feel the need to be loved by another breathing entity?

A young woman is always told, "You never need a man to make you happy."

So why is it that I feel like this infant child. This lonely thing that can only have happiness when another human being cares and loves how I care for him?

This emptiness I feel is not an everyday thing. While

I'm sure this emotion breaths and lives in my bones, it bursts out and **wraps its lethal arms around me**, and I feel like a weak individual.

To depend on another human being is not something I am proud of, but isn't that what a relationship entails: to compromise, love, and support, to feel as if you are never alone?

So why am I the one stuck with **Niagara Falls** coming down my precious skin? At moments when it's least expected, I regret them because who knows if his precious skin weeps for me?

A friend once said to me, "And, girl, stop that! You don't need nobody! That's how it feels for a little bit; but then, you realize it's so much better being single!"

Single. One. Individual. Apart from another ... this label I am unfamiliar with ... now isn't that just sad?

I came into this world alone, so I should be used to it right? **Wrong** because **single**, to me, is an anomaly. It's unheard of and, if I am, it's not for long.

While I need to be this, every bone, every vessel, every hormone, every cell in me is screaming the opposite ... **BE TAKEN.**

Be taken by **you**.

I've taken a million chances. Probably more and the one chance I had, I blew.

I tried again, and I still have yet to know the outcome. Sometimes I don't care that I received no response because I let my emotions out. I couldn't hold it any longer. He had to know what my **heart** was saying.

And sometimes ...

I do care because I feel as though if he felt how I feel, he'd be there.

If not, then I'll move on, eventually.

You live, and you learn.

But right this second,

I want to be PLURAL.

ME AND YOU.

PART II
Who am I?

It's All About Me

10/6/10

I am an open book.

I learn from my mistakes, and I advise others to do the same.

I am not a perfect person, but I am a perfectionist when it comes to school work.

I am an athlete who pushes herself to be the best she can be.

I am a Leo.

Strong-willed, caring, and passionate for those who mean the most to me.

Never have I given up on a friend or a loved one because I wouldn't want the same done to me.

I am a miracle baby.

Born 1 pound 4 ounces on July 28th when I was supposed to be born in December.

You do the math on how many months that is.

I am constantly on the mind of my family members because I was not supposed to survive, but I always tell them ...

I am a survivor. I will be successful. I will make them proud. I will accomplish my goals,

Because I ...

Will be the best I can be.

The next two poems "It Makes Me Sick" and "Cold Hearted" are strong and in no way, shape or form do I still currently feel this way towards my mother. Like most young adults there comes a time where they want to "spread their wings" and I felt at the time our relationship was not the best. Please don't read this and think or assume I ever hated my mother. Our relationship has grown, as these poems were written years prior. I always will love my mother and all she's taught me. There is nothing that can change that.

Jordan Freels

It Makes Me Sick

12/22/10

It makes me sick.

Those were your words the day you expressed your feelings to me about me staying with my boyfriend, but that's not even the purpose of this piece.

It makes me sick how you have so much control over me when I'm not five years old anymore.

Don't you think I can make my own decisions in life? You've taught me well; I know what to do and what not to do.

It makes me sick how you always think I have an attitude when nothing is wrong. I can't stand it.

I truly believe the "mother/daughter" lovey-dovey

relationship we once had will never happen again. You act like nothing I say or do is right.

You catch an attitude when things aren't done your way or when I don't do something your way. If it gets done, then what's the matter?

When I'm not here, who washes the dishes and cleans the house? The times I did come home, it didn't look like you did anything! But I bet you, if I were home, it'd be, "Jordan, do this … blah, blah, blah."

I'm so sick of not getting along with you. I'm sick of how you treat me sometimes. I'm sick of how you get so sensitive when I say or do something, and it offends you in some way when all I do is ask.

I can't take it anymore.

I truly feel like when I get older, you'll barely see the family or me I hope to have because of all the stuff you put me through.

It makes me sick to think I could be like you when I grow up.

I'm not you, and I hope to never be you. It makes me sick.

I dread the day it happens. If I do become you, I hate the fact that I could be.

I'm my own person; let me be me and not 'little Karen.'

My name is Jordan, so let me be me and stop aggravating me so much.

It makes me sick that I can't stand to be around you for a long period of time because 'it's always something I do or say wrong.'

Ever stop to think you could be the one who's in the wrong?

It makes me sick that you can never be wrong.

It makes me sick, all of this stupidness.

Cold Hearted

1/8/11

I must be a messed-up person.

I must not have a heart.

I must only care for everyone but you.

How can you even think that? You are my mother.

I admit; we do not always get along. Maybe sometimes I say things, and they come out so hurtful. But do you honestly think I have that much bad blood in me that I'd want to hurt you?

Sometimes you annoy me so much I don't like being around you, which is why I rarely come home. I'm not trying to be grown like you once said to me.

Sometimes you just don't let me breathe. I fear I'll

be like you when I become older, and I have control over my adult life.

I truly feel we clash so much because we don't understand each other; you don't understand how I am with my friends, why I say or do things, and I don't understand your humor, or why you do the things you do. When you touch me, sometimes my skin crawls. I'm not sure whether we don't get along because my father's not around or if that's how you see it.

I sometimes want to have a huge argument with you because then, you'll truly know how I feel. But every time, I stop myself. Why? Because I'm not so cold-hearted like you think,

I actually care about you. My mother. What a shocker.

Color Me

1/3/14

The depression and sadness had a hold on me. I felt like nothing else mattered. I just wanted to curl into a ball and stay in that position forever.

Grey is the color I'd use to describe that feeling. Even though sometimes that cold feeling overcomes me, I know that it is the brightness and support of God.

White won't let me reach that point. Every day is a new day, and my White represents a fresh start.

COLOR ME WHITE.

Because I learn from all the bad experiences I've had, and I see not,

Red for anger,

But my White because I learn and grow from each experience. Coming into this world, I fought. I literally should not have taken a breath. I was so undersized. But I am here, and I am strong.

COLOR ME GREEN.

I've overcome so much. I grow like the grass, like tree roots lifting up from the earth.

COLOR ME BROWN.

The stuff that does not matter.
Brown the in-between shade, the middle shade,
Dark Brown, a complexion I'll never be.

I'm the complexion of Yellow.

>Bright.
>Sunny.
>Golden.
>Sensual.

My Yellow shade gives me life; I smile in this shade. I laugh like I have not a care in the world shade.

COLOR ME BLUE.

A color with multiple shades.

Navy Blue for the days I just want me time,
Color me Royal Blue for the love I have for my, oh,
So Sweet Zeta.
Dark Blue for the days I just want to be left alone.

This Blue is almost close to that Grey but not quite! My Grey shade will never dissipate; it'll just fade away when I've hit that rock.

COLOR ME ORANGE.

The quirky, outgoing, somewhat adventurous, me. Not many get to see. Not even me. I've sheltered this shade for reasons I cannot explain. If you knew me well enough, you would know I'm more serious at times, letting my guard down is rare—almost impossible.

COLOR ME BLACK.

The years I grew up fatherless and resenting any man that came between my mother and me.

I've grown out of that stage, even without ever knowing or connecting with my biological father.

Who needs him?
When I have a DAD.

My stepdad, everyone says we resemble each other.
And this makes my heart sing.

COLOR ME PURPLE.

Sweet.
Adorable.
Naïve.
Genuine.

My Purple and my Yellow make me Brown.

My Brown comes after my Yellow.

My Yellow right in the middle, between my, oh, so sweet Blue.

My Yellow in the middle of my Blue. My middle shade was what, Blue? Yellow? Brown?

My multi-level shade, Blue.

But does the significance of each shade even matter?

I am these colors. These colors are me. In no particular order did I purposefully, piece this piece.

These colors are who I am.
Who I was, and
Who I will become.

PIECES OF ME

I am these colors all the time.
And while every shade may not show,
I know that to get to know me,
You must understand these colors
And to understand these colors means,

COLOR ME ALL SHADES.

Running Thoughts

1/6/14

My fear of writers' block.

My fear of not being good enough, of not touching people or making a difference.

Slight paranoia.

My grandmother's illness.

My estranged relationship with my biological father.

The relationships I've been in.

How I wish I could ask my father a million questions, all of which would begin with why. But I have no emotion when it comes to him.

I made a resolution a year ago that I would call him but never did. I wonder if it's worth it considering his illness, or what I have diagnosed him as a pathological liar, which scares me.

How will I know what the truth is?

How can he support and love his other children but not me?

The scenario in my head that constantly plays of me inviting him to my wedding and him not participating in anything; he'd just be a guest and watch my stepdad hold me against his chest for our father-daughter dance.

The only person to ever truly understand, besides my mother, how I felt, I no longer speak to. It's funny because he, too, went through the loss of someone he was close to. And I would think he would understand and sympathize, but that's neither here nor there. He was gonna be my savior, my knight in shining armor, but how could he when he barely had a connection with his own father?

Fatherless Man

1/6/14

Dedicated to my mother for always being there, playing both parenting roles.

Trying to come up with an emotion for someone, who was never there, is pointless.

Why and how, you say?

Because I never got one day, one explanation, one reason why he just up and left without saying goodbye.

Twenty-two years you missed, and I'm sure you'll miss more.

And I honestly can't say I care.

I wouldn't even try to open up that door,

Even if you were begging and pleading for me to listen.

For what? Why?

What could you possibly have to say now that I would honestly give two shits about?
You were never there.

In my mind, the man who I've grown to visualize is not the man in the pictures.
He is my father, but where is the proof, you say?
I have none besides my mother's words, and the bit she has explained.
She doesn't even waste her breath anymore with trying to paint this picture.

She's wasting her time and mine.
You do not exist.

I am NOT daddy's little girl—that picture was never painted.

Mama and I used to joke that you saw me come into this world and left for the store.

How sad.
How sad and pathetic you are.
You are not a MAN.
Correction, you are not a FATHER; at least not to me.
I have no connection to you, except biologically!

And that's farfetched for a man, who should have loved and cared for me, but you don't even show an ounce of regret. I could scream for all you put my mother through—the lies and deceit.

Was anything true?

If you ask me, I think you're crazy. There are too many stories my mother told me that just don't add up.

I think you're a pathological liar, so why waste my time trying to build and grow with a man who lies?

And who has probably been lying his whole life?

I know when I was young, and I didn't understand that I would cry to my mother and ask for a MAN.

A man who should have been there to help his child.

I cry writing this, and these tears are damn sure not for you.

They are for my mother, my FATHER, because she's raised and taught me what not to do.

Her fears and worries because I am her baby will worry me crazy, but I'd rather have that than a MAN who NEVER took care of his baby.

Do you know how many times I've seen my mother cry?

When she's shared stories with coworkers and close friends about how I was supposed to die!

I should not be here.

I was born prematurely. I'm quite sure you knew because somehow, you were able to make it to the delivery room.

Did you even hold me?

Kiss me on my cheek?

Look me in my big saucer eyes, because I was so frail, and tell me that you loved me?

> I doubt it. And I'm not surprised.

How could you?

Why would you?

When you were living a lie!

Do you know how much you missed?

Graduations, my first steps, even my first kiss.

I cannot help the tears that fall as I write this because I know the pain my mother went through. Every night, I would ask why my FATHER wasn't there.

And every night, she wouldn't know what to say.

I'm sure deep inside she wanted to die because she couldn't explain to her little girl that the man who was her father had not a care in the world.

At least not for me. And even now as I've gotten older, I will never understand WHY!

Why not love me?

And you had another family; another lie my mother discovered. And the nerve of your wife to have the nerve to write my mother!

And talk about how you never wanted her or her retarded baby.

You, B! God doesn't like ugly; I hope you pay for that mess.

I am far from retarded. I made it, and I am here!

How dare you question my intelligence when I was only a child. I did not ask to be brought into this world, but my mother and your sorry excuse for a husband made me.

If anyone's retarded, it is YOU for thinking you could be happy with a man who probably deceived and lied to you, too!

You think you won because he came back to you?

I know you are a sad, sad woman if you think that's the truth!

I won! My mother won!

Because she is free.

Free from this man who she thought would be there, but he just disappeared.

A man who had NOT an ounce of FATHER in him, not for me, someone so beautiful.

> Why didn't you pick me?
> Why lie and leave and cause all this pain?
> It will never make sense; I am tired of racking my brain.

I cry for my mother because she had so much pain, I can only imagine the questions she had. We were all supposed to meet one day, and I was finally going to talk to you, but then another lie came about. You were sick, or whatever had occurred; I hope God heals you because, if not, you're gonna burn.

I have your number and for what? What would I say? I wouldn't even know how to address you, probably by your name

Lamont.

How could you?

Why would you?

Why did you never seek me?

To see how much of a beautiful, young woman I've become. But you did nothing; you stopped at that door.

You are a coward; you are a sorry excuse for a MAN. My heart is in pain for all the memories you missed and made my mother handle.

How would you even explain yourself?

What could you possibly say that would justify why you did what you did. YOU HAVE OTHER KIDS.

Do you not understand?

I should matter!

I should get the same love and affection; instead, I was neglected, abandoned, and pushed to the curb.

To you, I mean nothing; I am nothing, and it is truly sad. I often think of you, Dad. And I use that word lightly because you are not it. I dream about it sometimes—making amends, waving the white flag, and maybe, just maybe, we could have a relationship. But honestly, I want all of this just so I can invite you to my wedding when I get older, SO YOU CAN SEE WHAT YOU MISSED.

If only you knew how much joy and satisfaction I get from that one little scene, maybe someday it won't be a dream. And if you ever get that far, if you're ever so lucky, I hope you realize at that moment that YOU MEAN NOTHING. Not to me. Not to my mom. Not to anyone. You were the one who left and missed out on so much.

You, Lamont, will never be blessed to know how smart I've become, what my fears are in life, and what I wish to do when I come into my own. YOU don't get that privilege. YOU DO NOT matter.

A man who cannot support one of his own for whatever reasons it may be, or whatever reasons makes sense in your sick head, you are not A FATHER. Do you know what a FATHER is defined as?

    No? Well, let me enlighten you.

A father is a male parent; a man who exercises paternal care over other persons; paternal protector or provider.

You, sir; you sorry piece of shit are certainly no

FATHER. You are lucky I gave you the title of DAD, MAN, and even to address you by your first name.

What made you think you could care for your other children when you forgot about me?

You are not a FATHER by any definition. You, to me, are a FATHERLESS MAN.

Don't know what that means? Well, let me tell you what I defined YOU as:

A person who is neither a man or a father.

That is what you are.

Congrats!
You've won!

You've earned a proper title that actually fits you—since being a FATHER and a MAN was too complex for you to get through.

Living Silently

7/24/14

I'm just not going to say anything anymore.

To speak my mind doesn't even matter, and maybe sometimes it is how I say things. But if I'm supposed to be treated like an adult, then why can't my opinion count?

I'm just going to keep quiet because when I say something, I come off a certain way; and when I don't say anything, I'm too weak, or I'm too quiet.

So, from now on, I'm just going to be silent.

I'm not going to say a word. I can't help if I say something and someone takes it the wrong way. I did not tell you to be in your emotions or not even listen to what I have to say.

Silence, something I need to acquire. Don't open my

mouth to discuss every little thing, every small situation, what I think of someone's opinion, or a question asked of me.

Silence from here on out is the best option for me.

I clearly haven't lived enough or experienced all in this small world I live in,

So, from now on, I'm living silently.

Tired

8/1/14

Tired.

Just so damn tired.

Of wasting my breath on people who essentially don't even matter, not anymore at least.

See, where there was once a full flowing beating heart is now an ice cold hole for people, who said they were going to be there for me but ended up killing my soul.

They hurt me because they were always supposed to be there.

But never took the time out to show an ounce that "they cared."

I just want to be loved. And that emotion is long

gone; no longer will I love someone who comes in and out of my life when it's convenient for them.

See, I used to think sometimes maybe it was me who needed to change.

But then I realized, no way. There's no way it can be me.

I feel like it takes common sense to be connected to someone emotionally.

Granted, don't get me wrong, that's not all it takes. But how can I connect with someone who acts so fake?

Who contacts me when it's convenient for them, or worried about everything that's irrelevant to my well-being.

What about me? Don't I matter? Why don't you ask about me? Instead of always being concerned about minuscule, materialistic, and unnecessary things.

Honestly, to keep it one hundred if I distanced myself, you probably wouldn't notice.

You'd assume I'm just being distant, but that's not even half of it.

PIECES OF ME

I wonder why I put in so much effort to make this relationship work.

For someone who loves and cares for me but won't take the time out to make sure I'm solid.

I wish you would pay attention.

Open your eyes, and clean out your ears because, after a while, I won't be here.

I'll be gone from your life, and you won't even notice.

I'm tired of talking; I hope you were listening instead of being so blinded.

If you missed it again, oh, well. I'm tired of wasting my breath again.

I'm going to live my life and finally decide to just not be bothered.

Masterpieces

8/5/14

My skin is beautiful;
Like a hot summer day, I am a yellow complexion portrait with a thin frame.

I am fragile.
The world is my canvas, and I want to paint masterpieces with my words.

My yellow skin glistens when the sun shines down on me like morning dew on a small blade of grass.

My skin is smooth like poured concrete and as cool as a summer's breeze.

Every inch of me is a blank canvas—from the top of my head to the souls of my feet.

Are you listening?

Do you understand me?
Everything on my person is unique.

My skin is beautiful;
And every which way I walk, the way my hips move back and forth, and the gap between my legs raises questions to those who don't know me.

No—I am not promiscuous.

I am just bowlegged. But even this slight imperfection is a stroke of color, and the paintbrushes are my words that roll off my tongue.

From my hair to the scars that I bare from being too small when I was pushed out into this big world from my mother's womb—it is there I always feel safest—nestled under her like a little baby bird.

My skin is beautiful;
And I am a yellow portrait with a thin frame just trying to be noticed with the poems that I create. The canvases that were once blank are filled with color.

Something to admire. Something to be proud of.

My skin is beautiful;

Like a hot summer day, I am a yellow complexion portrait with a thin frame.

I am fragile.
The world is my canvas, and I want to paint masterpieces with my words.

Same Old Same Old

10/19/15

I hope that when I get older, I don't shut down like I see some adults do and not communicate.

As I've grown, I feel like I'm slowly progressing with knowing what to say, how to say it, and when to say it.

But sometimes, you have to suck it up and speak.

Get out of your feelings, come out of your shell and say how you really feel.

Stay positive. Don't dwell on the negativity because that'll only cause more pain.

Pain that nobody needs, but if you keep that pain in, it will only boil over; and the outcome is never good.

Talk it out because communicating will save you all the heartache and pain you'll have from not speaking.

All it takes is a few sentences or more to lay it out on the table and talk.

I'm not perfect. I don't always say what I feel because there are times when I feel like it won't matter. So why waste my breath? If I can't have an adult conversation with someone, then I'm honestly just going to shut down.

Which I know only makes the situation worse, but until I feel like I'm being treated like an adult, I guess I'll keep my mouth shut. But doing that only makes me want to scream because it's not solving anything.

Either we can talk it out like adults and move on, agree to disagree, something, but eventually, I'll completely shut down and won't want to move on.

So, we'll be stuck with nothing accomplished but having only one thing in common, pain.

I'm so tired of the same old, same old.

PART III

Love Is

Love Is

4/9/12

Love is two hearts beating as one.

Love is the goosebumps you get when your significant other gives you that look ...

Of reassurance

Comfort

Passion

Guidance

Love is a commitment to be true and honest with one person.

Love is a struggle that has ups and downs because it is not perfect.

Love is the smiles, joys, laughter, and memories two people share.

Love is bliss.

Simple Chick

1/5/13

A simple chick can sometimes be labeled a silly B.

Society makes it seem like a young woman with goals and dreams can't be worth a thing.

> Now that's simple.

In today's world, only 'bad' females and video vixens get all the love. Cool, but then why slander their name if all it takes to earn fame is to bust a nut?

I guess everyone needs love, too? No matter what the cost.

Why can't a simple chick be put on a pedestal?

She has goals, goes to school, has dreams of making it big, but stereotypically, all she'll probably do is get an education and have a few kids.

Now, what's wrong with that?

But don't let her be pretty because then she'll be 'high sadity'

A woman with class, who doesn't have to show her ass to get attention, uses her brain.

But I guess beauty and brains doesn't even matter anymore.

Unless the beauty is a dime and the brain she gives results in a baby daddy and some kids.

Do you get it?

A simple chick does not mean dumb, or stupid; this definition is voiced when asinine people think a simple chick can't get anywhere in life if she doesn't use it.

Do you get it?

Or was that too simple?
Do you understand me?
Or are you just reading?

A simple chick is someone worth fighting for, not someone to be deceived and used, to be cheated on with a 20 percent female when the simple chick is the 80.

Now, what's wrong with that?

The good ol' 80/20 rule. Do you get it?

Don't give away something good for something that's not rare. That simple chick is the diamond in the rough who will always be there if she's treated right.

She's the exception to the rule.

A simple chick never gets the respect she deserves, and it's truly a shame because she's the one who changes the game.

She's the one who shies away from the drama and the petty foolishness.

She's the one who "doesn't exist" because all she is, is a "simple chick."

Pay close attention 'cause you just might miss her.

She's something special, but people never notice 'cause they always diss her.

She's too plain.

Jordan Freels

She's too boring.

She doesn't give it up.

But why can't she be valued just as much?

Secret

2/5/14

Kiss that spot that makes me squirm. My heart.

Your lips on my heart mean your lips on my bosom. While that'll feel good, I want you to

Love me.

Hold me because I feel safest in your arms. Don't let go, keep holding on, indefinitely.

I secretly think I love you.

But I keep convincing myself I love who you are, what you do for me, and how you make me feel.

So when we do say our first I love you's, it'll mean everything to me because I've loved you the longest.

Longer than the longest breath I've taken.

I secretly think I love you.

And I wish I could tell you, but I'm nervous about how my honesty will make you feel. Even though I can hear you saying, "You are never a bother to me."

It's not that I'd be bothering you, but what if I say I love you first, and you never love me back?

I'd be crushed.

I secretly think I love you.

But I keep convincing myself I love who you are, what you do for me, and how you make me feel.

I secretly think I love you.

Shower me with kisses, massage me into an erotic state, so the only thing that turns me on is your breath, your mouth, those three words I want to hear.

I ... love ... you.

I secretly think I love you.

But I keep convincing myself I love who you are, what you do for me, and how you make me feel.

Life Lessons

2/9/14

It's funny how life lessons can teach you so much. How in young boy's minds, all they wanna do is fornicate.

Excuse my bluntness, but these dudes think with the wrong head, sometimes.

It's ironic how young ladies, us women, want that thug life man in our life, at least some of y'all do. But if you think with your head like these young men do, you'll understand that you're more than just a screw!

Life lessons, man, they sure are funny. When you're young and naïve, you have not a care in the world until you hit adulthood, and you have the weight of the world on your shoulders. From stresses, to love, to finding the right one, wondering if you'll ever succeed and surpass the life lessons that were given to you in your adolescence.

You ever wonder why certain things just seem to happen in your life?

Like why God has blessed you with intelligence, but it doesn't matter much if you don't use it. Thinking with your brain is absolutely the most attractive thing.

If you can stimulate someone with your mind, and not with your curves or tongue, like really have an intellectual conversation, and not just talk about simple things—I promise you that's all it takes, at least that's part of it.

Stereotypical Love

2/13/14

Love. I want that forever love.

Give me your last, and I'll give you the world love.

Never will you have to question the love I have for you.

I haven't felt in love in so damn long; I honestly wouldn't even know what to do.

Would I be infatuated?

Would it be like puppy love?

The last time I was in love, like really in love, like I put everything to the side and thought about you every second, every minute, every hour kind of love … I can't even remember.

I want that never sleeping alone kind of love.

Wake up and know you'll always have my back kind of love.

I want that "black is beautiful love." You know, that "stereotypical kind of love." That "love is so beautiful, so real, so taboo kind of love." When the two individuals are "black kind of love."

Why is that?

What makes "black love so beautiful?"

What happened to loving somebody that's not your same race, your same size, or gender?

I can't even lie, though, "black love," is beautiful, but I want that type of love where skin tone doesn't define how you should care for your significant other.

All love is beautiful, "black love," especially for me, "interracial love," because that type of love is beautiful, un-stereotypically, "so unique," "so different," and "so out of the ordinary."

Love. To love someone means you give your all. You love someone with all your heart.

Love hasn't changed; that light still shines the same.

The only difference is I want mine to shine a little brighter!

I want my love to shine so brightly; it makes others eyes hurt.

Because while I won't have to flaunt or brag about how "real" my love is,

I know for me, it'll mean so much more because my light will never dim.

I want the right person to walk into my life so that we can connect as one.

So our heartbeats will be linked with each other's soul.

I want that stereotypical love where we won't let go.

That Special One

3/11/14

If you loved someone, would you entertain other men?

Would you do the same if it was just lust?

You want to be "wifey material," but when you're not with your "main," you portray a side chick mentality.

Why waste time with someone who does not want to be with you?

Don't you know you have someone who's willing to do all he's not? But you want to sit around and wait and hope he changes.

This fantasy world you live in is really upsetting. You're worth so much more, but you want to settle because you think you're gonna be with this man forever.

If you really thought about it, you would have been left him alone. But you think because you spread your legs, and you have years of a "situationship" that things will change.

Yes, you two have trust issues, and both did wrong. But if you haven't progressed, why are you still there?

I understand he's the love of your life. But he should love you in his life, at all times, not just when it's convenient for him.

Don't you know you're worth so much more?

Stop running to different guys knocking on that door, "of boredom," "just because," "just to get a quick nut." His sex game should just be a plus; it shouldn't be a factor.

He should want to be with you for who you are and what you can do for him mentally and emotionally, not for what you can do physically.

You should be treated like a queen, not pushed aside like you mean nothing.

Have some strength, pick yourself up off the ground, and run, run as fast as you can.

Run because you're tired of being second place.

Because you're tired of having tears run down your face.

Because you're tired of not being loved.

Because you're tired of not being that special one.

Being What We Want to Be

7/19/14

You were the only one who had my attention in that short period of time we knew each other, and it was blissful.

I haven't been that happy in a while.

Every time we hung out, I looked forward to it because when I was with you, nothing else mattered. No, seriously, I know its cliché-ish, but I never wanted to leave you.

You kept me sane, and you made me laugh. You made me feel, man—I can't even describe it.

All of a sudden, things changed, and I figured you would still be there because I felt like I needed you like I needed air.

Like who you were as an individual, as a living, breathing, human being—you kept my heart beating.

I remember exactly when we met, January 5. But we didn't officially hang out until January 17.

Who knew our love for words would attract us to each other, but sadly, your words hurt me when I least expected it.

Now you pop up like things are okay; now I'm the one who needs my space.

I am irritating, and I play the victim, those were your words, words really can hurt people, and I never thought you would be the one to hurt me.

I need time to see what I want to do. If I want to move forward.

We may be in different places in our lives, but that shouldn't stop us.

From being what we want to be.

726

7/21/14

I'm glad we had our talk; still, I can't help but think negative thoughts.

Even though we've expressed how we felt, is it crazy of me to start having doubts?

Love has nothing to do with it, even though it still feels so surreal.

We both were scared to say the most important words for any relationship to seem real.

I promise I won't bring up a relationship anymore.

I just want to be with you in any way I can, even if I can never become your queen and you my king.

And as I sit here and contemplate and my eyes tear with fear,

I don't want to pick up where we left off if neither person is "here."

And what I mean when I say this is that I don't want you to feel doubt or worry in any way.

I'm going to be here for you the same way I was when I was back home.

Nothing on my end is going to change.

I'm going to care and now, love you the same.

Be faithful to you, supportive, and make you happy; I can only pray you will do the same.

I know this will be hard, but I believe in taking this chance. A chance for us to grow.

Not having you in my life will only make me feel so small and unwanted.

Will you take this chance with me?

I'm glad we've started anew. I just hope you'll stay true like I plan to always do for you.

I want to continue to make each other happy because like I told you before, being around you gave me life. And I know for you, you said your heart was empty because you felt alone. So why not take a chance and grow?

I love you, babe.

Bare Skin

7/29/14

You have my heart not because of love but because of how you make me feel.

And even when I have my worst of days, I just have to think of you, and I smile.

You make me happy because you truly care.

So, when you see me, undressed, and bare-skinned, it's not to get a rise out of you; it's to let you know that even in my purest form, I only want you, your smile, your touch.

Showing you my bare skin is another way for me to express that I want to make you happy, and not just sexually, but mentally, physically, and emotionally, too. I'm showing you my bare skin because it's the last layer of my heart.

I'm showing you my bare skin because it's the last way I can express how I feel within.

Fairy Tale

9/3/14

I keep picturing this fairy tale of what you and I once had, and I question every day about how things ended so bad.

For someone who once said their actions played a part as to why I wasn't theirs,

I still don't understand how things went wrong.

Apparently, your "love" wasn't so strong.

I took a step back and tried so hard to reevaluate myself to be a better me, for we, but then that became too much for you. So I tried to follow your lead.

I slightly always felt like I was putting more effort in than you, at least toward the end.

And it's crazy how in the beginning things were great.

But then all of a sudden, you needed your space. So now I'm walking alone.

Being in love but not being loved is probably the worst feeling ever. But it comes in second to me trying every day to be better, and nothing seems to matter.

Everyone has flaws; I know I'm far from perfect, but all I really wanted was for us both to give our all and really make this "worth it."

After our last encounter, who knows what happened? Even when I apologized, there was no confirmation from you to let me know you truly understood how I was feeling inside.

You see, there's nothing worse than pouring my heart out in hopes for a change to acknowledge I made a mistake. So let's fix it, so we can continue to build this because my heart can no longer take this pain and hurt that it's being filled with.

From January until May, things were okay.

PIECES OF ME

From May to June, things became rocky.

And from June to August, we were nonexistent.

I promised myself I wouldn't reach out to you because I raised my white flag, and I apologized.

And if you really care and love me like you say you do, you would check up on me to see how I was feeling for someone who "was your lady."

It's been days since we've spoken. Every day I think of you less; I love you less, but I'm not going to lie—from time to time, you cross my mind.

But then, I think about from January to August and all we've been through.

Would it hurt to see how was I doing?

Or is that too much for you?

Do you remember when you said, "Now there's a hole in my heart."

Because of you, now this is how I feel. I just don't understand how things went so wrong to the point where we don't even speak.

I can't help but question;

Jordan Freels

Where did we go wrong?

Hopeful

2/1/15

Every relationship, I try to learn from it.

But you, you were different.

I thought we had something, and I am not bitter. I am not upset. I am just not in the mood to be hopeful.

See, I told you what I told you because I meant it.

I don't think about the past because it makes me sad, and with you in particular because you were my last. I don't know if you still feel anything like I do.

Okay, so we spoke, and we understand each other's

side. But I still can't help but wonder what if things ended differently?

But then I feel hopeful again. And it's not just you; it's others, too. You were just the last person I gave my heart to, so it's still bruised a bit. Even though I've prayed and moved on, I guess I'm not over it like I thought. I'm still hurt.

But it's okay. I stopped crying myself to sleep. I don't wish to hear from you or hope that I will and never do. It's way past that point because we're on good terms now. I just don't think of the past too much because I am just not in the mood to be hopeful.

It ended. And that's okay.

But I'd rather stay where we're at and continue to be friends than waste my time and energy thinking about the past.

I learn something from every relationship and being hopeful just doesn't fit.

Dream Chasing

10/24/15

I've seen you before; somewhere in my dreams.

God, I thank You for this perfect human being.

You were someone I prayed for, and I can only ask that I'm what you need.

And now I'm blessed to know you.

Know you in a way that even still amazes me.

Every day I learn something new from you and every day I etch it in my memory, so I can think of you when we're not together.

Which is always never because I've only seen you in my dreams.

This perfect human being you are.

But it's crazy because sometimes I see you. You know, random places like the park, on the street, at a store, and I wanna shout to you.

"Hey!" Start a general conversation so I can know you better each day.

But then I remember, you won't recognize me. We can't speak; we can't talk about our day, our fears, or our dreams.

But that's when I see you. When I'm dreaming; when my breathing has slowed, and I'm lying down. Stressed or happy, angry or elated.

Every time I close my eyes, you're the one I'm anticipating.

Tell me that my day is going to be okay. Be my positive inspiration, my ray of sunshine when the world seems so gray.

The one I crave to just stare at. Look into your eyes and have my whole-body fill with happiness.

I want to know everything about you. You're my best friend, and I don't even know your name.

I want to know every imperfection, every flaw, every

negative because I know when I close my eyes, and I see you, you know everything about me.

I've accepted who you are and I don't even know you. Tell me your name so I can stop dreaming.

When my eyes are closed, and I can see you, I know things are okay. And, yeah, I know things won't be great all the time, but that's just how things work in a relationship.

There's good and bad, right and wrong, and ups and downs; but all I know is your queen is waiting for you to help her fix her crown.

Tonight, I'll close my eyes and tell you about my day, but let me first start by saying,

"Hello, it's nice to meet you, again" ... if only I knew your name.

Reflections About My Best Friend

2/13/16

It's sad I feel how I do because you really mean a lot to me. The best friend I never had; the one who never judged me but loved me like a best friend should.

But sometimes, things seemed to take a turn for the worst; and then, we'd stop speaking.

We both knew that drove us crazy. In the end, we'd be friends again, and things would be the same.

But I'm starting to feel like I'm the only one always to blame.

And no relationship should be like that whether it's platonic or romantic.

So maybe we should call it quits if things are just too rocky.

Just know you'll always be in my heart and prayers, but I'm tired of feeling unloved, unappreciated, and not listened to.

You're going to do great and be great but just without me.

I love you.

And know that if you ever need me, I'm only a phone call away. But I doubt you'll ever take that chance because you say you think about me and miss me all the time. So why not take the step, just talk it out, and we move on?

I guess that's not your nature. I'm just tired of being stepped on.

A best friend doesn't treat someone they care about like this, so whenever you're ready to finally speak up, I'll be here. I just hope it's not too late for your sake.

I can only do so much to try and be your friend. If the feelings are not reciprocated, then only one of us will be left hurt in the end. And by then, it'll be too late.

A Beautiful Mind

5/30/16

You ever just be impressed by someone's presence?

Like their physical being just has you star struck. Then when you actually get to know them, they impress you with their intellectual thoughts.

Like their intellect is just so beautiful.

Their mind is what's so attractive to you that nothing else seems to matter. It sounds cliché, but I just can't help but to want to know someone for more than just the physical.

Stimulate my mind with your intellect; match your mentality with mine so that we can have dope conversations about nothing and everything under the sun.

Let's grow brain cells together and teach each other things that only we can understand.

Can we just stare at each other and be comfortable in that space?

Your intellect impresses me, so let me just stare at you while you talk.

Sometimes I like being the one to listen.

I Wish

2/20/17

Why is it that at night I think about the one thing I spend all day not thinking about?

That out of all the time in the day when I'm alone that thought comes to my mind.

I hate it.

It's like a never-ending tornado. I do so much in the day that you're not even a thought.

I wish I could sleep until your memory just fades away.

I'm sorry.

I can't keep thinking about you when I know you think of me less.

I wish our story was written differently. I wish our experiences and our memories were different. So that way, I could change the ending every time, and let it be something happy and warm instead of me feeling empty. Instead of me feeling hollow. Instead of me feeling like a never-ending tornado.

Why do I think of you at night so often? I wish your presence wasn't even present. I just wish the story was different.

I wish I would listen to my own thoughts when I tell myself, don't think of you so much. Focus on me.

But then that just fails, and when night falls, you crawl back into my thoughts.

I wish you weren't there.

Dear Black Man

7/6/17

Dear Black Man,

I pray for you.

Every day you're shot. I'm scared for you.

I hope to bear a young king one day, but I'm terrified to raise him in a world that is threatened by our skin.

I want to tell you to run. But then, I realize running will only have you not breathing.

Or standing still will have you not breathing. You won't be able to ...

Tell your mother you love her.

Tell your father you love him.

Kiss your children goodnight.

I value you. I cherish you. I love you.

I'm scared to think a black man doesn't even stand a chance.

Why can't you just make an honest living? And not be threatened by someone who thinks they hold more power over you because they carry a gun and they're a different race than you.

Dear Black Man. Being black means, you're already dead to them.

You don't matter. You don't exist.

And that makes me sick.

Before It Even Began

9/25/17

I told you everything about me, and I still ended up alone.

I thought things were so good until all of a sudden, they weren't.

I'm empty and numb now. I'll question everything someone else tells me because I trusted you so much.

I keep telling myself to push through and stop thinking about you, but I can't.

How do you tell someone all of a sudden you don't want to be with them anymore? When just hours before, you were willing to give me your last name.

I want to believe you, but it's hard to. Yes, I said

I trusted you with everything, but now I feel like nothing you said was honest.

Were you just playing me? And how can I trust your words again when the thought of us not being together hurts the most?

Do you even love me?

You have me so confused.

I just wish I knew your truth.

Before you, I was different, less happy, less Christ-centered, and I thought I made you happy, too.

And who knows if you'll even respond to this poem. I just needed to write something down, get it off my mind.

I really hope and pray you weren't just thinking with your emotions; and in due time, you can be mine, and I can be yours.

But I guess until then, our love story ends.

One Accord

10/17/17

Sometimes I guard my feelings, so I don't seem so weak. Even though, in all honesty, I always want to repeat the cute stuff you say back to me like,

"I am so glad to have you in my life."

Or when you say things like …

"I am the luckiest guy in the world."

To that, of course, I'll say, "Yes, you are. Any man is lucky to have me."

Sometimes I just get scared if the lucky one is you.

You send me all these memes of what you say is our "relationship goals."

I can't lie, I've sent you a few or two; but then, I start to feel like,

Is this real? I haven't felt like this in years, and you say you feel the same. Do we feel whatever this amazing thing is, is so real that its meant to be?

I don't even know if I believe in fairy tales anymore.

I just believe in you and me.

I believe that we've helped each other grow.

I believe we've bettered ourselves.

I believe that you are the man I have been praying for.

For the man who keeps me grounded.

For the man who helps me breathe easier.

For you, I'll do whatever I need to make it work.

I just want our stories to be the same.

Shattered Sunshine

2/1/18

Stop giving life to things that suck the life out of you to begin with.

You cannot grow when you're withering away.

Your well being, your sanity is more important than giving your all to situations that don't matter.

This pit in the bottom of my stomach should not be here, this knot of intertwining lies, tears, and deceit should not be here.

This feeling of feeling unloved should not be here, it's like snakes crawling all over my body.

My bones are fragile like glass being broken and my feet are walking over them, stumbling over them, tripping over them, trying to get you to love me.

I'm constantly cutting my feet on these glass shards trying to stand tall, trying to walk as quickly as I can to have a voice that says...I am here.

Notice me. Love me.

I am broken.

I feel like a little girl who doesn't know which direction to go.

Like a child who wants to be loved but no one is giving them attention, so I find other things to distract me.. like,

Oh look, the sun. Look how bright it is and how it makes me feel. The sun is like the love I never received from you.

The sun showers me with affection and keeps me warm at night, something I never even got to crave or to even miss from you... because you were never there.

I am here. Do you see me? Does the sun blind you or will I constantly have to keep walking over glass shards of hurt and pain and sorrow just so you can continue to not love me.

I can't keep hurting myself to make you see me. I have to love me first, so I'm taking the right path this time.

I'm walking on solid ground where glass shards can't cut me. I'm choosing me because choosing you only cuts me deeper each time. I am strong on my own two feet, and the scars that I bare from you will disappear sooner rather than later.

PART IV

Short Stories

11/24/10

Nothing written here is what I am feeling. I just decided to do something different, so I chose to put my mindset as someone else. None of these characters are real, but their situations are. All the characters are different.

Character 1

You ever heard that phrase, "I'm sick and tired of being sick and tired?" Well, that's how the hell I'm feeling now. I'm sick and tired of taking care of these babies when his lowdown, dirty, self doesn't even help. I'm sick and tired of having them cry all the damn time, and I cannot figure out what is wrong with them. You know, sometimes I feel like just pretending I'm insane and kill them all, so then I don't have to deal with their mess, and everything will be solved. I know if I do that, I'll end up in a mental institution.

Stop, because I know what you're thinking; only a real crazy person will even think about pretending to be crazy. Well, maybe I am, but who cares? No one has ever diagnosed me, so how should I know?

What I should have done was not have any damn kids because no one is helping me. My family just completely deserted me—so much for family is forever. That's BS. I'm just sick and tired of living where I live. The home in my head is beautiful. No gunshots, no ambulances, none of it.

You must think I live in the ghetto?

Bingo.

Don't ask me how I am still able to pay for my bills. I think I'll be kicked out soon. I don't know where I'll be then, probably in a shelter. But that'll be best for me. Don't get me wrong; I love my kids, but they're so needy, always crying and stuff. When is someone going to take care of me?

I'm sick and tired of not having a steady job, always getting fired because I'm late, or I did something wrong to 'jeopardize' the company. But whose fault is it if my babysitter comes late? Not mine! At least I show up to work, even if it is a few hours late. I don't know what these damn people want from me. I just wanna say, "Listen, Mr. White Man, forget you. No one wants to work for ya behind anyway. Peace out!"

You must think my name is Mrs. Sick and Tired, huh? Wrong, my name is Kadisha Caramel Davis, and this is my story.

Character 2

Daddy says if I say anything about how he touches me, I'll get in trouble, and he'll just beat me more. At school, my teachers notice and sometimes, I can't lie fast enough. So that just means I get beat even more when I get home. I wish mommy's angel would listen to my prayers, so she could make daddy stop.

I miss mommy. Daddy took her away from me. Daddy used to beat mommy, too. But mommy went to heaven because she had an accident.

I wish I could fly and live somewhere else, where daddy couldn't touch me. At night, I cry. I rarely sleep because I'm scared he'll come to my room like he sometimes does. Daddy wasn't always like this, and I always try to remember how it all started.

Daddy's coming into my room now, and I have nowhere to hide. My room is but so big, and even if

I did hide, he'd find me and probably beat me for not being visible.

I hate him. I hate him so much. I wish he was dead.

Ten minutes elapse, and the story continues.

This time, daddy tries to talk to me before he starts touching me. He says, "Gina, come here, baby. It's okay; don't be scared." When I don't move, he yells, "Come here, little girl! What did I say?"

I quickly move in fear, knowing if I don't, he'll beat me and molest me even more. After the beating, he puts his fingers in places they shouldn't be and rubs his hands on places so tender and innocent, I close my eyes and pray he's almost finished.

You wonder why I haven't said a word to anyone, I presume. It's because I feel like no one can help me but myself. When the time is right, he'll get what's coming to him. I know I'll be the one inflicting the pain.

Karma's a you know what. When I have the energy, she'll be my best friend. We'll overcome this monster, whom I once loved.

Gina and Karma, best friends forever.

PIECES OF ME

Character 3

My name is Sophia. I'm a high school senior, and I'm on my way to New York University (NYU) to become a film major. I have a good life, and for that, I am thankful because I know my family and friends are always there to support me.

My best friend, Gabrielle, and I have been like sisters since the diaper days. Sometimes she acts like she doesn't even know me, and I don't know why. She'll ask me if I remember hanging out with her a specific day, and I can't remember. We joke around that I have short-term memory loss, but sometimes, I feel it's something deeper.

Sometimes I misplaced things, and I didn't know why. For example, I would put my computer on my desk and leave my room. When I returned, it would be on my bed.

Fifi did not get along with Sophia; she was the evil

portion of her. She controlled Sophia from not doing her homework; and then, she would get in trouble. One time, Sophia didn't do a huge paper for history class, and Fifi ruined it for everyone.

Tina was the child inside Sophia. She came around whenever Sophia got in trouble. Tina sometimes argued with Fifi because she knew what Fifi did was wrong. For example, Sophia forgot to wash the dishes like her mother asked. When she got in trouble, Tina surfaced, and replied, "I'm sorry, Mommy. I'll remember next time, promise."

Her mother thought it was odd Sophia responded the way she did, but all she said was, "Okay, dear." Her mother thought to herself, *Sometimes I wonder about that girl.*

The day of Sophia's history paper, Fifi emerged. Mr. Turner asked, "Sophia, do you have your research paper?"

Fifi responded, "No, but I'd like to have you, Mr. Turner. I see the way you glance at me during class." Mr. Turner turned red and asked Sophia to see him after class.

After being scolded and returning to school the next

day, Mr. Turner approached Sophia again. This time he approached her in a more sexual manner, and said, "Sophia, what you said to me in class was true. I do have a sexual attraction to you, but because you verbally announced it in front of the class, I had to scold you. Good trick, huh?"

Sophia was taken aback and tried to distance herself from Mr. Turner; but then, Amy appeared. Amy and Fifi did not get along. Amy felt Fifi tried to shine the light on her and take her position as the sexual individual. They constantly argued back and forth. After bickering, Amy had the last say and made a sexual advance toward Mr. Turner.

Another student caught the interaction between Amy and Mr. Turner, and eventually, the school faculty heard of the news. Little Sophia was expelled from school, and Mr. Turner was fired. Her family and her best friend, Gabrielle, had no understanding of how things happened. Her family was shameful, and Gabrielle eventually distanced herself. Before she finally left the state, Amy, Tina, Fifi, and Sophia all got in touch with Mr. Turner one last time.

Amy's short letter read: Enjoyed my time with you, Turner, maybe I'll see you later on in life. Don't forget about me.

Tina: Mr. Turner, I don't know how this happened or what happened exactly, but Sophia was not who you thought she was. I can't explain it. I'm sorry this happened to you.

Fifi: Guess my smart remark got the ball rolling, huh, Turner. If Amy weren't there, I would have shown you a better time. That's a promise.

Sophia: Mr. Turner, I have no recollection of that day. I am completely ashamed and embarrassed about what happened. Please, believe that girl you ...well, you know, interacted with was not me. Words cannot describe how sorry I am and how much pain I've caused you. I hope one day you can forgive me. You were truly my favorite teacher. I learned a lot from you.

Mr. Turner received all the letters from each and was confused on who or what these people were saying, besides Sophia. Sophia struggled with who she was. Tina, Fifi, and Amy still lived inside of her, and would forever have control over her until Sophia's able to control them herself. These were their stories.

About the Author

Jordan Freels is the youngest of three children with older twin sisters. She lives in Virginia Beach, Virginia, although she was raised in Maplewood, New Jersey. Before her move to the south, she obtained her Bachelor of Arts degree in English with a minor in Journalism from New Jersey City University. She's always loved to read and write as a young child.

Her dream is to write children's books. She is currently working as a special education teacher's assistant; and is presently enrolled at Old Dominion University to obtain her Masters in Special Education. Her love for children with special needs has grown since working in the school system, and she hopes to continue to love and teach the children of our future.

In her spare time, Jordan loves to spend time with her family, spoiling her nieces and nephews, doing crossword puzzles, and blogging as much as she can. Her blogging website is JordansJargon.com.

www.ingramcontent.com/pod-product-compliance
Lightning Source LLC
LaVergne TN
LVHW051057080426
835508LV00019B/1930